ALLIANCE, ILLINOIS

Other Books by Dave Etter:

Go Read the River (1966)

The Last Train to Prophetstown (1968)

Strawberries (1970)

Voyages to the Inland Sea
(with John Knoepfle and Lisel Mueller; 1971)

Crabtree's Woman (1972)

Well You Needn't (1975)

Bright Mississippi (1975)

ALLIANCE, ILLINOIS

Poems by

Dave Etter

KYLIX PRESS / ANN ARBOR

Published by

Kylix Press
1485 Maywood
Ann Arbor, Michigan 48103/USA

These poems first appeared in the following publications: *Abraxas, Ann Arbor Review, Ark River Review, The Chariton Review, Chicago Review, Chicago Tribune Magazine, The Chowder Review, Cincinnati Poetry Review, Cottonwood Review, CutBank, Dacotah Territory, December, The Dragonfly, Epos, The Far Point, Focus/Midwest, The Greenfield Review, The Harrison Street Review, Hearse, Hiram Poetry Review, Icarus, Illinois Quarterly, The Kansas City Star, Kansas Quarterly, The Lake Superior Review, Midwest Quarterly, Minnesota Review, The Nation, New: American & Canadian Poetry, North American Review, Northeast, Northern Lights, Oakwood, Open Places, Pebble, Poetry Northwest, Poetry Now, Prairie Schooner, Quartet, Raccoon, Rain, Rapport, River Bottom, The Salt Creek Reader, Salt Lick, Shenandoah, South Dakota Review, South Florida Poetry Journal, Sou'wester, Stinktree, Sumac, Tennessee Poetry Journal, Three Rivers Poetry Journal, TriQuarterly, Uzzano, Wells Elevator, Wind,* and *Wisconsin Review.*

The following poems appeared in *Voyages to the Inland Sea: Essays and Poems by Lisel Mueller, John Knoepfle, Dave Etter,* edited by John Judson (La Crosse, Wisconsin: Center for Contemporary Poetry, 1971), pp. 61, 68: "Emmett Beasley" (as "Man Talking to Himself") and "Clarence Fowler" (as "Mr. Fuller"). Copyright © 1971 by John Judson. Reprinted by permission.

Library of Congress Cataloging in Publication Data

Etter, Dave, 1928–
    Alliance, Illinois.

    I. Title.
PS3555.T68A8   811'.5'4   78-14560
ISBN 0-914408-08-9
ISBN 0-914408-09-7 (pbk.)

To the memory of my mother

JUDITH GOODENOW ETTER

(1894-1944)

But I'm interested primarily in people,
in man in conflict with himself,
with his fellow man,
or with his time and place,
his environment.

—William Faulkner

. . . there is nothing more native than speech.

—George Ade

In the end a man can expect to understand no land but his own.

—Vachel Lindsay

CONTENTS

ALLIANCE, ILLINOIS

GEORGE MAXWELL: County Seat

Pushing deep into Sunflower County now,
just minutes before sunup,
the big semitrailer truck droning on
in the breezy, dew-heavy darkness;
leaving behind the cornfields,
the red barns, the windbreak trees,
snorting by the city limits sign
announcing ALLIANCE, pop. 6,428,
thumping across the railroad tracks
of the Chicago & North Western,
slipping past roadside produce stands
and hamburger and milkshake drive-ins,
bouncing and rattling again
between the bruised bodies of billboards
saying where to shop, eat, sleep,
where to fill up with gas:
LICHENWALNER'S DEPARTMENT STORE,
CARL'S MAINLINE CAFE,
HOTEL TALL CORN,
BOB'S TEXACO;
dipping toward the polluted waters
of the sluggish Ausagaunaskee River
and the once stately section of town
where neglected Victorian houses,
with their cupolas and wide porches,
are set back on maple-shaded lawns;
remembering good and bad times,
lost faces, half-forgotten names;
and then the driver taking a last drag
from his Marlboro cigarette,
poking me in the ribs
with yellow, tobacco-stained fingers,

one letter of Jesus on each knuckle,
breaking the long silence between us
by saying over the asthmatic breathing
of the great diesel engine
that we are here, this is it,
here's that town you've been asking for;
moving slowly into the Square,
with its domed and clocked courthouse,
its bandstand and Civil War monument,
its two-story brick buildings,
lawyers and doctors above,
the town's merchants below;
stopping on Main Street
next to the Farmers National Bank,
stepping down to the curb,
thanking the driver for the lift,
grabbing a U.S. Army duffel bag,
slamming the cab door with a loud bang,
then turning around to face
ALLIANCE CHAMBER OF COMMERCE
WELCOMES YOU
TO THE HYBRID CORN CAPITAL OF AMERICA,
and thus knowing for dead certain
that I'm back in the hometown,
and that nothing has, nothing could have
really changed since I went away.

SAM BUCKNER: Lovers' Quarrel

As I gaze at it in the summer twilight,
the moving face of the Ausagaunaskee River
is not the face of a drowned boy
who went wading a little too far
with cane pole or hound dog,
nor the face of the drunk from out of town
who fell off the railroad bridge one spring night
after losing at poker, or was it pool?
No, there are no haunting faces here,
no one to remember, no one to grieve for.
But back beyond weeping willow shadows,
a gravel road, and withered catalpa blossoms
is the face of an unhappy country girl,
wet-eyed now over a packed suitcase,
hoping to catch the next bus for Mattoon
so she can tell Mama and Papa
about the mean mouth she got married to.

ROGER POWELL: The Talk at Rukenbrod's

I sit in the shade on the high curb
in front of Rukenbrod's grocery store.
I sip a cold Nehi grape and listen to the talk:

"You remember Andy Gump, don't you?"

"My blue jeans are too tight, she tells me.
I feel creepy walking past the Square
with all those dirty eyes scraping my skin."

"No, I never knew Nettles. He was an Elk."

"Sure, Paul was farming in Pickaway County, Ohio,
but he got going in this spiritualism stuff.
Goes all over now, West Coast and all."

"Butterflies, you know, taste with their feet."

"The wife took the kids down to Hannibal,
Mark Twain's home town on the Mississippi.
I told her to bring me back a nice souvenir."

"Joe Palooka I remember. My brother Jake liked him

"Nettles ran a forklift up at the cannery.
Then he was with A&W Root Beer, nights.
Heart attack it was. In Terre Haute, I heard."

"A purple martin eats 2,000 insects per day."

14

"So I think I got me a modest daughter, see.
But last week I catch her with another girl.
And they weren't playing no dominoes, neither."

"Fred's cousin was formerly with Dial-a-Prayer."

"Guess what they brought me from Hannibal?
A Becky Thatcher back scratcher! No lie.
I didn't know whether to laugh or throw a fit."

"Butterflies do what? Taste with their what?"

I take my empty into Rukenbrod's grocery store.
They have run out of Nehi grape.
I grab a Dr. Pepper and sit down again.

"You sure you don't remember Andy Gump?"

RICHARD GARLAND: Railroad Strike

The radio says
the trains aren't running
for another day.

When the railroaders
go out on strike
in the dead of winter
the frozen ground
of northern Illinois
loses its iron music.
Folks who live near the tracks
get a little jumpy.
Something familiar
has been switched off.
There is nothing now
to hold together
the body's old rhythms.

A thin, stooped woman,
wrapped in a heavy muffler
and blowing white ghosts
of zero-degree breath,
slams the back door,
flips away a cigarette,
and tips over a basket
of 30 or 40 green bottles
into an empty oil drum.
The noise is like a bomb.
Across the way shades fly up.
A man slips on the ice.
Thirteen dogs bark wildly.

A blizzard wind
rattles the windows
of the abandoned caboose.

FLORA RUTHERFORD: Postcard to Florida

What brightens up this prairie town in spring?
Not tulip, not dandelion, not willow leaf,
but New Holland, Massey-Ferguson, and John Deere.
Right, the brand new farm equipment
glistening now in the rooster-strutting sun.
And oh what colors they have given us:
strawberry-red, sweet-corn yellow, pie-apple green.
A fragrant breeze drifts in from the plowed earth.
The excitement of crops seeds my furrowed brain.
Mother, we have come through another wintertime,
and I had to write and tell you this.

HERSCHEL NIEDERCORN: Requiem

Aunt Pauline was a bright lights girl:
the kind who likes hotel lobbies, noisy bars,
opera night, New Year's Eve on State Street,
and a steak approximately the size of a doormat.
When she knew she had only a short time to live,
we brought her out to the country:
muddy roads, bare locust trees, frozen lawns,
a barn full of Holstein cows, lots of kids.
She stayed in the house all winter,
telling us stories about her many travels,
playing hearts and dominoes, reading Sherlock Holmes.
By spring she had lost a lot of weight,
and I knew the worst was soon to come.
We took one last ride in the Dodge pickup:
waved to the rowdy Callison girls
singing "Rock of Ages" on their screened porch,
stopped by the creek, watched the squirrels play.
Tonight she kissed Benjy, our youngest boy,
who said, "I can belch anytime I want to."
She died upstairs in the sewing room.
She said, "I touched the sun on a red flower
and it was cold, so terribly cold."
Aunt Pauline was a bright lights girl.

TUCKER STONE: Stuttering Hands

The broken-down barn of a man,
his face an Appalachia of ruts and gullies,
leans against the weathered bricks
of the Farmers National Bank.

It has quit raining again.
The high school boys coming up Main Street
break into a runaway gallop.
They are wild horses drunk in a green wind.

Approaching forty, I realize
that I am really terrified of growing old.
Already the buxom farm girls
are aware of my stuttering hands.

CLARENCE FOWLER: Nuts and Bolts

Now what's a *Farm Journal* doing in a doctor's office?

Look, if I could only point to a tractor
out in someone's cornfield or in the barnyard
and announce with an authoritative voice,
Say, there's a Massey-Ferguson 1130:
Perkins direct-injection diesel engine,
turbocharged 120 horsepower,
hydrostatic power-steering,
air conditioned cab, air-luxe seat, etcetera,
it just might make my mechanically-minded son
sit up and take another glance at his old man.

Think hard: Do I know a nut from a bolt?

And then, if I could go on to proclaim,
ever so casually, you understand,
Hey, take a gander, will you, at the brand new
New Holland 1469 haybine mower-conditioner:
37 horses, water-cooled engine,
and a sickle bar that can cut hay
at 1,520 strokes per minute,
the boy might even forgive me somewhat
for being Sunflower County's leading seller
of women's dresses and women's hats and shoes.

Should I study up? Is it too late to learn the score?

SUSAN COBB: Names

I want to be Susan Jonquil,
a bold springtime flower
sticking out of a jelly glass;
or Susan Ferris Wheel;
or Susan Television,
my bare tummy warm with loud pictures;
or Susan Blueberry Muffin;
or Susan Iuka, an Indian girl
sparkling in beads and silver rings.
But more than anything,
I want to be Susan Mississippi,
a river that does what it wants to,
and any time it wants to,
moving south past fish and funny boats,
past moonlit towns and hooting owls.
And Susan Honeysuckle
would be summers of fun;
and so would Susan Lemonade
and Susan Lawnmower.
Look, I'm telling you right now,
being plain Susan Cobb
is no great thrill to me.

PIKE WALDROP: For the Record

The telephone poles have flowered with posters again:
WALDROP FOR SENATOR and I LIKE PIKE.

I sit here in the White Star Pharmacy these days.
Let my old cronies yammer at the Square.

She said to me, my daughter's little daughter,
"Grandfather, they named a big clock for you."

Three thought Lincoln the best, four favored Roosevelt,
but I stuck up for Herbert Clark Hoover.

I have a gold railroad watch in my vest pocket
and a democratic hole in my right shoe.

I'm against taxes — usually; war — generally;
and sin, suffering, crime, and cor-ruption.

There are some traditional American smells here:
root beer, bacon fat, a good Tampa-made cigar.

Out at the dairy farm I have six stuffed owls
and a huge Cal Coolidge campaign poster.

The Republic is all I ever worried my head about.
Where is it now they bury the bones of circus horses?

BRUCE PUTNAM: Crayola

It was just a child's
crayon drawing,
but perfect somehow:
broad blue prairies
soaking in mist,
a lightning tree
still supporting
a rope swing,
and in the foreground
a bushy dog
asleep on a hill
of sycamore leaves.

"And where am I
in your picture?"
I asked her,
tugging a yellow braid.
"Oh, you're not here,"
she said, sadly.
"You've gone away
to Cincinnati,
dreaming of me
lost in a brick town
with too many weeds
and fences."

DEWEY CLAY DOYLE: Sleeping Bags

We have a resurfaced road smelling of tar,
a black-eyed susan that escaped the grass fire,
a harp of willow leaves playing the same old tune.

Beyond a field of Shetland ponies cropping red clover
the morning sun reddens six barn windows.

I have lived around here all my life.

By the yawning mailbox I yawn again
and try to rub the night crumbs from my eyes.
Then when my ride comes along and stops,
I gather up a heavy lunch pail,
a thermos of Thelma June's strong coffee,
and *Wild Horse Mesa* by Zane Grey.

Another working day, another day to go to work.

In twenty-two minutes I'll be in Atlas
to help make some more sleeping bags.

My name is Dewey Clay Doyle.
You can see it right up there
where I spelled it out with care on the water tank.

ZACHARY GRANT: Guilt

We drive to Chicago's Union Station.
I say goodbye, give her a quick kiss.
My Nancy Lee is going off to New Hampshire.
We never got along. I'm glad she's gone.
But then, back home again, it hits me:
I saw only her faults, her blemishes.
After brooding over a few whiskey sours,
I stumble around in a blues funk.
The neighbors put away their porch swing.
A truck dumps coal at the fuel company.
Sad and alone in October's smoky twilight,
I walk through the black walnut trees.
Across the broken limestone wall, I see
rusty soup cans, a discarded water heater.
A squirrel scampers among dry leaves.
The empty birdhouse darkens on its pole.
Far off, a freight train blows at a crossing.
The wind turns cold. I think of snow.
Well there's not much more I can say.
I was always right. Now I'm wrong.
I know it's no picnic being a father,
but if you have an ugly-duckling daughter,
close your eyes and love her to death.

YVONNE WYNCOOP: Looking at Clouds

I am looking at black rain clouds
and a patch of bright blue sky
the exact shape of Illinois,
a state where my crazy Aunt Minnie
spent her whole life saying,
"Aren't we ever going to move from here?"
Look, the patch of sky is looking
very much now like Delaware,
a state my aunt never heard of.
And a good thing, too, since that's
a place she would have raved about,
what with all those historic houses
and first families with family trees
rooted among the dank bogs of England.
No, she would have never shut up
had she known about Delaware
and the thin green mists they have there,
her bony finger tracing the map
eastward out of Sunflower County.

RANDY WHITE: **From a Big Chief Tablet Found under**
a Bench at the Courthouse Square

Katy will only kiss me now
when we crouch among
the tall cornstalks
off Potawatomi Road.

I think she thinks she's
Pocahontas,
hiding from the gunshot eyes
that would scorch her flesh.

Last night in a hugging fog
an Illinois state trooper
roared up the blacktop
like a wild beast on fire.

Katy bit her sore lip,
and it bled
and bled
on mine.

PRUDENCE ARCHER: Thirteen

There are girl dreams I can make out of snow,
always using this house in snowfall December,
a wedding cake house with pretty me in a snow-white dress
ready to descend the staircase and disappear in snow,
off to the snowy Episcopal Church and my wedding day.

These snow-cloud dreams of marriage vows and bridal cakes
have been going on for many snowball winters,
although I'm just thirteen and my snow-hating sisters
were married not in snow but in May, June, and September.

I'm Prudence Archer and I believe in snow.

DAVID MOSS: Corn and Beans

You won't believe it, Uncle Max.
The corn is already scarecrow high
and those beans are swelling up,
proud as new granddaddies.

What we have here, my boy,
is some good old-fashioned
ag-ri-cul-ture.

Corn wants to fly away, Uncle Max,
and beans want to spread their fire.

Son, the sun is surely gospel.

JOHNNY WILCOX: In the Barbershop

He spits tobacco juice
on the baseball news.

I stick chewed bubble gum
in the comic books.

He wears a greasy hat
and pants with no belt.

I wear a snake-head ring
and socks that don't match.

He comes hot from corncribs
cussing out bankers.

I come damp from poolrooms
talking down hustlers.

He was a circus bum
who wrestled a bear.

I was a shoeshine boy
who married a whore.

He's done two years in jail
and clobbered a cop.

I've gone to reform school
and flattened a priest.

They know us in this town.
We kick up the dust.

WALLY DODGE: The Hat

He sure had a mess of fishhooks on that hat.
Of course he didn't have it on his head,
because he was still working, working hard,
still on duty at Fred's gasoline station.
No, that hat of his was there on a telephone book,
right under the rack of highway maps.
Yes, I picked it up and looked at it, yes,
but not to look over the fishhooks.
It was the hat itself I was curious about,
having never seen a yellow hat with a green brim
and wanting to see what the label would tell me.
Who stole the hat is something I couldn't say.
I don't fish myself, and the hat didn't fit.
So I spent the rest of the day looking at tires
and watching a Jaguar get a grease job.
Say, is there anything special about that hat?
Maybe those fishhooks were made out of silver.
Or maybe the hat was imported from Peru.
I know it's no big joke to you, you being his wife
and having to live with an unhappy hatless man,
but I can't cry about it now, can I?

STUBBY PAYNE: Stocking Tops

In June the syringa bushes bloom,
and I swear that I can smell oranges there.
That was your smell, Bee. I knew it well.

And I think of you today in Farley's Tap,
where all winter long you sipped Gordon's gin,
legs crossed, showing a bulge of creamy thigh
above those tantalizing stocking tops.

Green summer again. Rain. The warm earth steams.

You left town on a Burlington day coach
to visit an aunt in Prairie du Chien.
"She is full of money," you said, "and dying of cancer."

Towards the end of July,
Sunflower County cornfields turn blond.
Stiff tassels shake in the sexual sun.
There's a dust of pollen in the air.

How many bags of potato chips?
How many trips to the can?
Oh how many quarters in the jukebox, Bee?

August heat. The girls go almost naked here.

Like some overworked Cinderella,
you always took off just before midnight
on the arm of Prince or Joe or Hal or Smith,
bound for your place above the shoe store.

Yes, I should have bedded down with you myself,
said So what if you were a bumbling barfly,
every drinking man's little honey bush.

FRANK TEMPLE: Wet Spring, Dark Earth

Hope

Wasting away in her bed of psalms,
my mother opens tired eyes to say,
"I'll be on my feet in a week or two."

Agony

She will have no doctors, no drugs.
The Lord is her shepherd, her trust.
But His rod, His staff don't comfort me.

Death

Here on April's tulip-trembling hill
the gravestones darken in the thin rain.
We stop at a fresh grave, a new stone.

Love

Sister Betsy, seven years old in May,
shows me her buggy of sleeping dolls.
"Every one of them is a mama," she says.

Memory

My father stands under a fragile moon,
pounding cold fist into cold hand,
his Donna dying in a gospeled room.

Faith

Deep in a green-bladed field of corn
I pray I may honor my mother's faith,
to know that in God there is no death.

CHICK CUNNINGHAM: Horse Opera

Cowboy movie with John Wayne!
And I have popcorn and my gun.
But I'm still in a jail of grief.
Some ornery dude rustled my bike.

Mary Lou is a pretty keen sis.
She pats me gently on the knee.
Squaws know when a kid is down.
John's horse just got shot.

It was plenty tough out west.
You had to be right on your toes.
John sure drinks a lot of beer.
Now how can I ride to school?

My pa gets madder than John does.
He may not listen to the truth.
Indians being nasty to whites.
Take that, and that, bad guys.

GARTH LIGHT: Muscles

I'm lifting weights in a sweaty barn.

Gail is a shy, flower-faced windmill
turning gently on a bed of air,
her long legs the color of goldenrod
under the strong and mating sun.

I'm grunting. I'm gasping. I'm groaning.

I'm Garth, her bulging lover,
a silo standing between horse and house,
steely-eyed, mute, but lovable,
a bruiser with massive thighs.

I'm building muscles I'll never use.

HERBERT TOMPKINS: The Crippled Poet's Dream

I was trying hard to write this long Civil War poem,
moving closer to the Battle of Wilson's Creek.

She was tired of her lime-green lollipop,
dropping it in a scramble of honeysuckle vine.

I was busy, wrapped in thought, deep in hot Missouri,
reviling all the wrong maps and regiments.

She was finished with her picture of the old house,
saying it was very sad we had to move away.

I was confused, blinded in a smoky cornfield,
losing my weapon, tearing my Yankee shirt.

She was digging a doll's grave for Hannah Minerva,
repeating that strange and musical name.

I was sure we were all dead now, lost in time's fable,
dreaming of leafy rivers under our sycamore tree.

GARY SHACKHAMMER: Remembering the Thirties

The clock ticks in the hall, ticks in the hall, ticks . . .

Roy's Model T Ford rusts behind the mortgaged barn.
Goldenrod grows through a hole in the runningboard.

Our daddy never did come home from the turkey shoot:
"He was last seen in East Moline," says the deputy.

By the Franklin stove we listen to Roosevelt speak.
We nod our heads and chew stale bread-heels with mayonnaise.

The morning westbound freight is loaded with men out of work.
Karl draws an NRA blue eagle on the calendar.

"Sew and sew: the whole country's gone to stitches," Ma says.
My pants are shot; Steve's coat belongs to Timothy.

Peggy's new buffalo nickel rolls down the storm drain.
Now there's nothing more that jingles in her piggybank.

Uncle Cornelius moves in with us in June.
In August we all move in with Aunt Winifred.

The clock ticks in the hall, ticks in the hall, ticks . . .

EMMETT BEASLEY: Man Talking to Himself

Brown cigars beat green cigars.

You are a fool out of Faulkner,
a farmer finding the general store closed.

Another game? Sure thing. Cut the cards.

She was an old and furious child.
I read that somewhere.

The piano smells like a coffin.

Forget the soiled shirts, the dirty dishes.
When the fog lifts we'll go for a spin.

Gone, the wife is gone and gone for good.

Man, easy on the Schlitz there.
Just three cans left.

Let's hear it now for bachelorhood!

MELISSA JENKINS: Staring into Winter

Big flakes of snow
fall on the last remaining oak tree leaves.
I love the dry, ticking sound they make
on this storm-threatening afternoon.
There should be an owl somewhere nearby,
tightening his feathers and staring into winter.
I know there are deer about,
for I have seen two of them cross the road
day before yesterday,
just up past the railroad tracks.
And where is the red fox
that jumped the barbed wire last spring,
hightailing it out of Ruby Cooper's chicken yard?
Snow in big flakes
thickens in the scrap of oak woods on the hill.
I have an empty house to go to
and cold thoughts to rattle in my head.
Pray for me, Father,
and for the deer whose gentle eyes
are the color of syrup bubbling in the pan.

PORTER KNOX: The Christmas Tree

Above Sam Kuykendall's dime store a loudspeaker blares
a never-ending selection of Christmas carols.

O little town of Bethlehem
How still we see thee lie,
Above thy deep and dreamless sleep
The silent stars go by.

Years ago, when I was the head of a large family,
before everyone either died or moved away for good,
we always had a brightly-lit Scotch pine or balsam fir
at Christmastime on the farm near Noon Prairie.
I remember the avalanche of presents, the happy faces,
the huge turkey dinners with candlelight and wine.

I shouldn't have done it, I guess, but I did it.
I went out into the teeth of a zero-cold wind,
walked up to the Christmas tree man at the A&P,
stamped my freezing feet in the icy parking lot,
and demanded to buy the biggest tree for sale,
having found thirty dollars in the tobacco-tin bank.
Oh, I had to have a Christmas tree on Christmas Eve,
and I was willing to leave a sick bed to get one,
willing to drag it back to my room on Illinois Street.

I will have to string popcorn to decorate my tree.
I have neither time nor strength to search for lights
or red and green balls or the soiled blue angel.
My old man's hands flutter like wounded quail.
I puff my pipe, cough, then slump to the floor.
A newspaper catches fire and the popcorn and the tree.

Still in thy dark night shineth
The everlasting light,
The hopes and fears of all the years
Are met in Thee tonight.

The fire engine screams through the tinseled streets.
Now no one can hear "Silent Night, Holy Night."

WADE HOLLENBACH: Hard Cider

"Can I come too?" she said.
I said nothing and kept on walking,
moving away quickly down the railroad track.
But one-eyed Billie June came,
and she grabbed my hand and grinned.
Near the bridge we stopped and looked
at the moonlit waters
of the Ausagaunaskee River.
For a minute, I forgot she was with me,
lost as I was in my faraway thoughts,
my troubles in finding a new job.
"What's in the sack?" she said.
I pulled out the tall dusty bottle.
"Hard cider?" she said.
"Hard cider," I said.
I screwed off the cap and took a long swallow.
"Can I have some?" she said.
I passed her the bottle.
She helped herself to three big gulps.
Her teeth were yellow, her dress was soiled,
and a hunk of coal-black hair
had fallen over her one good eye.
"Hard cider! " she said.
"Take it easy," I said,
"we've got a whole night ahead of us."
She kissed me smack on the lips,
knocking off my hat, dropping the bottle.
"Hard cider," I said,
and hurled a stone into the river.

VERNON YATES: Talking about the Erstwhile Paperboy
to the Editor of the *Alliance Gazette*

Mister, he was an awkward, gangly son of a gun,
and, if it's truth you're asking for,
just a little bit on the homely side, too.

He whipped around here on a battered blue bicycle,
making faces, doing tricks on the handlebar.
What a cutup that kid was, a genuine show-off.

He was kind of sweet on Penelope Sue for awhile,
until the Turner twins, Ted and Tod, put him straight.
They told him to go peddle his papers, and we all laughed.

The boy was sure reliable, I'll say that for him.
No one on Prairie Street ever had to beg the headlines.
It's a real shame he's dead, and so young.

He was with a patrol behind the enemy lines, it seems.
They got ambushed by the gooks and chopped to pieces.
That's all I know, that's all I heard.

Well, I'll always see him there in the old news depot,
rolling up those Chicago dailies and shouting,
"You'll never see me in any Vietnam!"

DR. MALCOLM LINDSAY: Catfish and Watermelon

All day we stared at the river,
in a boat blessed with fish luck
and this woman's enormous breasts.
Now, in a tiny clapboard house
hidden by willows and trumpet vines,
mammoth Millie fries channel cat.
"How do you like it?" she asks me.
"My new scarlet nightgown, I mean."
"You're a sternwheeler caught fire,"
I tell her, "a real conflagration."
She laughs and the floorboards creak.
Wonderful! — 300 pounds of female
shaking up a sudden summer storm.
When she quits it's time to eat.
Later, after the fish are just bones,
I knife open a ripe watermelon,
broad striped and thumping good.
Millie picks out a whopping piece
and goes to work with gold teeth.
The juice runs off her double chin
and trickles between hills of flesh.
She kisses me on my sunburned neck
and then bites a black seed away
that was sticking to my right ear.
She smells of islands in the sun
and old boats soaked in morning mist.
No, it's not half bad at all
to be in love with Mammoth Millie,
a river gal twice my size.

CHARLOTTE NORTHCOTT: Insomnia

The moonlight on this spring night is simply dazzling.
One thousand brides are dancing in white wedding gowns.

Sixty-four coal cars clanked over the rail joints,
clickety-clacked right into Alliance, Illinois.

The latest wedding pictures fill the weekly *Gazette.*
I read all the names and hate all the happy faces.

Every last coal car was piled high with lumps of coal,
which sparkled there in the frosty March moonshine.

But where is *my* lover, *my* dreamer of marriage feasts?
Is he asleep, a moonbeam kissing his collarbone?

O you seekers of true beauty, where were you tonight
when a whole trainload of diamonds danced through town?

POP GAINES: After the Farm Auction

I wanted to bring back some useless thing,
some utterly unusable, used-up thing.
What can you or I do with a butter churn
that will never churn butter again?
Exactly, you are absolutely correct, old woman.
Nothing, nothing at all.
Go ahead and laugh, make yourself sick.
So I don't know what I'm doing, is that it?
Did I buy the white china doorknob?
Or the mezzotint of St. Francis feeding squirrels?
For old times' and for pity's sake,
no I did not, nor the Boston rocker either.
The butter churn goes on the kitchen table.
Leave it there, leave it be.
Now then, when is the next farm auction?
I may be needing a coffee grinder next.

ISAIAH ROODHOUSE: Putting off the Encyclopedia Salesman

No, the wife is not at home just now.
Well, actually, she's home,
but she's back in our corn patch
picking out some ripe ones for supper.
With all the corn growing
in Sunflower County, Illinois,
you probably think it's a bit strange
we should want it in the yard too.
But the corn tassel, mister,
is my special, personal idiom.
I love to look at corn, eat corn,
and even think about corn.
What we have around here
is good corn air and good corn earth.
And you can hear corn growing.
Whispering, crackling sounds.
Cornstalks, corn leaves, cornhusks,
corn silk, corn kernels. ...
I'll call in the wife, if you want,
but she'll side in with me.
As I said, we have four encyclopedias,
and the other books we've bought
are near to taking over the house.

LUCY BETH YOUNGQUIST: The Reunion

After the turkey, oyster dressing,
cranberries, creamed onions, yams,
nuts, fruit, pumpkin pie, and coffee,
Father takes off his Sunday shoes
and stretches out on the davenport,
giving us strict instructions for
no singing, no dancing, no loud laughing.
He quickly drops off to deep sleep,
the unread society page tented
over his fat and snoring face.

The stuffed common barn owl
gathers dust in the attic now.
It finally made Father nervous
after all those years of saying,
"But I love him, he's good company."
And like this puffy-cheeked bird,
the relatives that have come here today
for our big Thanksgiving reunion
are sent to the limbo of "who cares."
Father likes to eat and be alone.

TRAVIS JOHNSTON: North

Haze hangs heavy in the slow September air.
A freight train crawls through parched cornfields
and past backyards strung with shirts and jeans.
A troop of sunflowers slumps across the fence.
The sour-mash sky around the collapsed silo
is the color of George Dickel's best whiskey.
Jake Cotton's barn says CHEW MAIL POUCH TOBACCO.
The bald brakeman leans from his yellow caboose
and, smiling, waves to me, and I wave to him.
Down in Tennessee I had many friendly fathers.
But I'm in Illinois now, on northern soil,
lonesome in the long shadow of Abe Lincoln's name.

ELLEN OPDYCKE: The Fall

The one-legged house painter,
my dearly beloved husband,
stands on the topmost rung
of a tall ladder that leans
against the whitest house
in Alliance, Illinois.
His cap, torn at the crown,
is spattered with brown paint
from the big job he performed
on Al Ackerman's horse barn.
But his coveralls are clean,
and a new red bandanna
hangs like a bright flag
out of the right rear pocket
where he squirrels his change.

The one-legged house painter
has been on that ladder
painting the same colonial house
for more than 22 years now.
Through my kitchen window,
I see him there every day.
Never mind the banker's wife
who fainted when he fell
and the screaming ambulance
that took him away to die.
Forget that the old mansion
was torn down last week.
And ignore, if you please,
that his favorite brush
is as hard as Rover's bone.

HAROLD BLISS: Questions and Answers

On my way up to the post office for stamps
I stop awhile in front of the pet store.
Heinz Kleinofen is on a wobbly ladder
washing his dirty, rain-streaked windows.
"Do you have any rabbits left?" I ask him.
"Bon Ami," he says, "you can't beat it."

Heinz is married to Bertha, a deep thinker
who thinks she looks like Ingrid Bergman.
Surrounded by eighty-six teddy bears,
Bertha always lounges in bed till noon.
"How's the good wife these days?" I ask him.
"Swedish," he says, "she can't understand it."

In June, Heinz decides to get far away.
He wants to see the Grand Canyon, alone,
to forget about Bertha and the pet store.
When he returns I inquire about the trip.
"Did you thrill to the big hole?" I ask him.
"Gila Bend," he says, "I can't believe it."

JOE SPRAGUE: Fourteen Stones

Late summer hollyhocks grow on both sides
of an ornate iron fence
that separates Indian Hill Cemetery
from a row of rural mailboxes.

The names on the boxes
have been carefully lettered.
There must be no mistakes made here.
Everyone wants what is coming to him.

Whipping up the yellow dust
on my way home for a bean sandwich,
I stop my dry-cleaning truck
to reach for a magazine and two gas bills.

In the crowded graveyard,
where lie the bones of four generations,
there are fourteen Spragues
carved on fourteen stones.

I'm no longer worried about bad news
concealed in flowered envelopes,
for my kinfolk are all gone now.
And my own fate waits across the fence.

DELBERT VARNEY: One-Way Conversation with a Rug Beater

Bam, bam, bam went the baseball bat.
Her pa was out in back beating a rug for his wife.
He had a neck like a wrestler and hair in his ears.
I sat on the lawn and chewed a blade of grass.
"Did you know I'm in love with your daughter?" I said.
Bam, bam, bam went the baseball bat.
The dust really jumped from that sad old rug.
He had a tattooed chest and a scar on his left cheek.
I sat on the porch and smoked a Lucky Strike.
"Did you hear I'm marrying your daughter?" I said.
Bam, bam, bam went the baseball bat.

NOAH CREEKMORE: Bingo

Because I have little choice in the matter,
I drive my silent wife downtown.
Stores on the Square burn night lights,
but the movie marquee is brightly lit.
"Fools' Parade," I say, my voice rising,
"a real humdinger with Jimmy Stewart."
She says nothing, grips her purse tighter.
We slip past FALSTAFF, REXALL, EAT
and turn sharply into South Fifth,
stopping at an ancient red-brick building,
with its scrolled cornices, its roof of pigeons.
The American Legion Hall is where we are,
where the town plays bingo on Tuesday nights.

And the voices are calling back and forth
in the cold-snap September darkness:
"Call me when you're ready, Cary."
"Wish me luck, Wally, lots of good luck."
"Don't spend the food money, Freida."
Car doors slam, shoes scrape the sidewalk.
My wife nods grimly, says "Same time, Noah."
I drive back toward the empty Square,
in need of male laughter, a dirty joke.
The Courthouse clock is lost in fog.
I pass up EAT and REXALL again,
but pull up to the curb at FALSTAFF,
the neon a warm and friendly glow.

DREW MANNING: Harvest Dust

The carnival rays of the sun
illuminated the dust clouds
that rose behind a blue combine
harvesting forty-two acres
of good Illinois soybeans.
I stood there quietly,
the evening breeze around my head,
watching the dust thicken,
seeing emeralds and red tapestries,
seeing golden showers of rain.
Then the sun dropped behind
the last stretch of prairie,
and once again the dust
became no more than dust
in the cool and farm-dark air.

ARDIS NEWKIRK: At the Charity Ball

For something to say, he said:
"I just love greenhouses and the steamy heat
and all those small plants growing tall there.
And I love woodchucks and gymnastics.
I can tell chicory from prairie clover.
Down by the tracks where Stacy Engle lives
there's gobs of it right this minute.
I know the names of all the townships
they have here in Sunflower County.
Not many people can say that, believe me.
Do you like player pianos? I do.
The Donovans next door have one, you know.
And they start it up every now and again,
and Mrs. Donovan makes loads of lemonade,
and we shoo the flies away and laugh a lot.
I can tell swamp frogs from tree frogs.
Sure, I think Black Hawk got a bum deal.
I also think it's a terrible scandal
they have discontinued Old Settlers' Day."

For something to say, I said:
"Harrison Stanley McIntyre, shut up.
You know I don't like to talk when I'm dancing!"

REV. FELIX DIETRICH: Gospel

I'm thinking about those
boot prints up and down
the kitchen floor,
a foiled bank heist
over in DeKalb County,
and the sermon I can't write
for Thanksgiving week.
Now what is *humble?*
And what is *grateful?*
I know what chickens are:
big thundering trouble,
at least when your son
goes off and steals one.
"You don't know turkeys,"
I tell him, kind of mad.
What I told the sheriff was,
"You got lawman's tracks
from your muddy boots
right up to my freezer,
I don't hold with stealing,
and as far as I'm concerned
Bob's a good boy."
My sermon on Sunday
is going to be one I stole
off this Okie preacher
during the Dust Bowl years.
It's here in the files
along with my clippings
of the Younger brothers.

KIRBY QUACKENBUSH: September Moon

The old houses, dusted with moonshine,
creak in the dry and dragging wind
that pokes about this town:
where potato salad and cold beans
are eaten in stuffy kitchens;
where, in tubs of tepid water,
ponytailed girls who love fast horses
slide pink soap between their thighs;
where skinny boys lift weights
in bedrooms gaudy with football stars;
where doctors read comic books
and lawyers read numbers on checks;
where sex-starved wives wait in the nude
for tipsy husbands to be bored
with beer glass and cue stick;
where children sleep like stones
and hall clocks tick and tock
and cats yowl and dogs growl,
as another hot Labor Day winds down
in the webbed and wrinkled dark;
and I, moondust on my face,
return from a long walk to the depot,
the depot of many fierce goodbyes;
and it's just this I want to say:
Luanne, my lost and lonely girl,
if you want me on this summer night,
run through the grass now and kiss me.

NELSON HURLBUT: Last Day of Summer Vacation, 1924

The yellow-dog sun rolled over again
as my brother and I, cheeks rosy as peach stones,
galloped cornstalk ponies toward the shady house,
each of us with a corncob gun
going *bang, bang, bang, bang, bang.*

And perched on our mother's grapevined porch
was the third grade teacher fanning her face
with a sumac-red spelling book,
her gray hair swaying like an orchard cobweb,
and she was shouting "Whoa, horse, slow down there."

Then our deep groans rose up with the dust,
we boys seeing that ancient schoolmarm
brandishing the dreaded speller weapon,
and we dropped corncob guns
and left our limp cornstalk ponies for dead.

FLOYD NYE: Dog on the Stairs

To live in the second oldest house
in Alliance, Illinois,
is to be aware of many ghosts.
Sometimes late at night,
when a storm is blowing the trees about,
I'll sit up in the big tester bed
and hear the very first man of this place
whisper to his good wife,
who is half-asleep in a lace cap,
"Is that the dog who just went *thump* on the stairs?"
And she'll scratch her right arm and say,
"It's only the wind, Willard."
But I'll get up and go see anyway,
even though 2:16 a.m. on March 2, 1853,
is a long, long time back,
and the last dog we had
died five years ago this month
under the wheels of a Mayflower van.

AVERY LUCAS: Apples

It's that time of year again,
and I grab my walnut cane
and take my string bag
off the hall closet hook
and walk down Grant Street
under a blowing rain
of yellow and russet leaves.
I pass a dozen boys playing
football on a muddy lawn,
pass sumac and grapevine,
pass front porch steps
orange with pumpkins,
pass smoking leaf piles,
pass Feldkamp's lumberyard
which smells of redwood planks,
pass the empty public pool,
pass the first farm west
where a monstrous corn picker
harvests a forest of corn,
and then come at last
to an abandoned orchard
of six scrawny trees.
Here, I gather the ugliest
apples you've ever seen:
puny, lopsided, bird-pecked,
yet possessing a special
flavor all their own.
And no one knows this,
no one except me, Avery Lucas,
and I'm not telling nobody
nothing about nothing.

GROVER ELY: Ancestral Home

Rebecca Ann, her head wrapped in a polka-dot scarf,
leans over the balcony and shakes out a patchwork quilt.

Down in the yard the sundial has died of too much shade.
But the white oak is a landmark, the town's pride.

All four chimneys are unsafe and haven't smoked in years.
Stepping-stones to the grape arbor are thick with moss.

I sit in the summerhouse, sip a glass of good port,
write in my journal, read the stories of Mark Twain.

Behind me, a creaky wooden gate shuts with a ghostly click.
Two or three red-orange blossoms drop off the trumpet vine.

Later on we will drink green tea and talk about the past.
On the piecrust table is a Bible with a golden key.

The ancestors who built this monumental brick home
still stare, thin lips pursed, from their oval frames.

We, the living Elys, are softer, poorer, sadder, but
we try to stay on another year, bear another Ely child.

HOWARD DRUMGOOLE: Hotel Tall Corn

You know, I sorta, kinda like it.

It's not very tall at all,
and the only corn about the old place
is dispensed by the night desk clerk,
who's been around since Alf Landon
stopped being presidential timber.

The beds are soft, the plumbing works.

If you miss the last bus out of town,
that's where you go to get some sleep.

One cold, gloomy December evening
I slogged through half-frozen slush
to attend a wedding reception,
held in the swankiest suite they had.
The next morning the groom was found
hanging by his farmer's red neck
in a round barn west of Rochelle.

Woody Herman's band played there once,
a real "Woodchopper's Ball."

I hope it stays alive a little while.

It's the kind of rube hotel
Sherwood Anderson would hole up in
to write about the beauty of horses,
the faded dreams of small-town girls,
and the lives of homesick millhands.

You know, I sorta, kinda like it.

BARNEY PRINGLE: Heat Wave

The house smells like we had smelly socks for supper.
Under my chair is no place for your roller skates.
I sure wish those cicadas would shut the hell up.
Movies, movies, movies, that's all you care about.
No, I ain't worried, a tornado would improve Elm Street.
My front name? Now what kind of dumb lingo is that?
Let your mother explain "opera house," she's old enough.
Go join the 4-H Club, it sure won't bother me none.
Don't call me a grouch, young lady, and I mean it.
What? You drinking another can of Green River again?
I'll sit here and sweat in my shorts if I want to.
Monday night, and I feel already I've worked a week.

CHARLEY HOOPER: Schoolteacher

Barefoot in the sticky June twilight,
I mow a patch of stone-jumping grass.

The girl next door makes a sick, throw-up face
and stirs her drum of burning weeds.

Across the street the retired switchman
hawks and spits on a ramshackle porch.

My son, a dirty diaper around his knees,
offers me one lick of his dripping ice cream cone.

I find a moldy tennis ball near the doghouse
and bounce it off old Butler's roof.

A big decision must be made soon:
grade arithmetic papers? or drink some wine?

There have been many nights like tonight,
many hours of what to do? where to go?

And wouldn't you just know this too:
the Pontiac has another flat tire.

JUDGE EMIL ZANGWILL: Angry Words

It's Friday night again in Alliance, Illinois.
I leave the Courthouse by the jail-side door,
drained from the endless bickerings of the courtroom,
the lies, the tears, the bloodlust accusations;
sick of sharp-tongued lawyers and dull-eyed juries.
On my way home, walking toward Liberty Street,
I stop at Bert and Larry's liquor store
to pick up a quart of Jack Daniel's black label,
then continue to plod along for another two blocks,
the April mist thickening to April rain.

My third wife, Dixie, has sued me for divorce.
Daughter Laura Jean has dropped out of sight
somewhere between the Robert Street bridge in St. Paul
and the Boatmen's National Bank of St. Louis.
Son Scott writes from Stateville that prison guards
have taken his poems, his notebook of new songs.

Yes, this empty house has heard angry words, too:
"cheat," "bitch," "I'll break your goddamn neck."

Gents, listen to me now and listen to me close.
Some men should always get drunk alone.

MARCUS MILLSAP: On the School Bus

I go up the steps of the yellow school bus.
I take a seat in back, and we're off,
bouncing along the pitted blacktop.
What am I going to do after school?
I'm going to make myself a sugar sandwich
and go outdoors and look at the birds
and the new fiberglass silo
they put up across the road at Mott's.
This weekend we're going to the farm show.
I like horses okay, but farming's no fun.
When I get old enough to do something big,
I'd like to grow orange trees in a greenhouse.
Or maybe I'll drive a school bus
and yell at the kids when I feel mad:
"Shut up back there, you hear me?"
At last, my house, and I grab my science book
and hurry down the steps into the sun.
There's Mr. Mott, staring at his tractor.
He's wearing his DeKalb cap
with the crazy winged ear of corn on it.
He wouldn't wave over here to me
if I was giving out hundred dollar bills.
I'll put brown sugar on my bread this time.
Out by the water pump the grass is soft,
like the body of a red-winged blackbird.
Imagine, a blue silo to stare at,
and Mother not coming home till dark!

TOM RANDALL: Under a Gigantic Sky

There's a milkweed butterfly
kissing Barbara Allen's knee.

Yep, I'm going to fall in love again.

We live near a burned-out roller rink,
the Chicago & North Western tracks,
and a field of tornado-toppled corn.

Barbara Allen sleeps in the shade
on the warm, pine-scented grass.

Oh, man, it hurts me so good.

We have been here forever in this place,
drifting under a gigantic sky,
lost on the golden prairies of America.

A breeze lifts Barbara Allen's skirt
above her hips, above her head.

Wow!

The whole damned Middle West
is looking
up.

KARL THEIS: The Widower Turns Eighty

Old November is novembering again.

Now whose blind and broken dog
is sprawled in that heap of brown leaves?

Somewhere beyond those dead elms
a pale woman calls my name,
but she doesn't mean me, no, not me,
for my name disappeared years ago
in a rush of November wind,
about the time I had my first stroke
and the last Burma Shave sign
was ripped out like a vile weed
on the southern edge of Sunflower County.

My body is a cracked cornstalk.
My face is dusted with crop dust.

November again and again and again.

NORBERT JOYCE: Drummers

Yellow-lit railroad coaches
and new towns at blue dawn
run through my memories.
I had a good territory:
the Dakotas, Wisconsin,
Minnesota, and Iowa.
I kept my sample cases tidy,
was neat and courteous,
and knew my products cold.
Believe me, sonny,
they respected your old grandpa.
What did I sell? you ask.
Medicines was my line:
stuff for headaches, asthma,
stomach troubles, hay fever,
even female complaints.
I knew all the hotels,
the depots, the boardinghouses
from here to Aberdeen.
Drummers were a special breed
back in them long ago days.
"Knights of the grip"
was what they named us,
or "commercial tourists,"
or "trade interviewers."
We were good at pranks,
told many a tall tale,
and were fresh as April dew
with all the country girls.
When the company went broke,
I sold cars in La Crosse,

then worked for Ward's
in Duluth and Des Moines.
But it was a real comedown:
no more good talk with friends,
no more nights in St. Paul,
and no more railroad coaches
with them yellow lights.
What's that again?
What are female complaints?
Well, boy, you see ...
I think it's time for bed.

JUNIOR IVES: Barn Burner

After Petersen's barn burned
on that warm Indian summer night,
we all sat around the kitchen table
and drank from a full-moon of apple cider,
saying "You did it, you did it,
you set fire to Seth Petersen's barn,"
pointing accusing fingers at one another
and laughing to beat the devil.
Oh, I carried on with the best of them:
with Ma and Cousin Annabelle,
with Leroy and fat Carl and Virgil,
with Uncle Roger and Aunt Alice.
And they never suspected me,
never knew why I was crazy for cold cider,
my throat parched the way it was
from the red excitement of flames,
from running across corn-stubbled fields,
my pockets bulging with matches.

LOUISE CATHCART: Hearing an Old Song Again

You don't have to tell me that.
That was "As Time Goes By."
And I know it was a great song
and once warmed up all
the cold kitchens and parlors
in this wind-bitten town.
I used to be happy
as day-old chickens
peeping in a splash of sun-dust
when I'd hear that love tune
on my daddy's new Philco.
But later on it made me sad,
because I'd remember the boy
who used to say to me,
his arm around my neck,
"That's our song, lover girl,
and don't you forget it."
Then, just like that,
he moved away to Sioux Falls,
and I never saw him again.
That was "As Time Goes By."
You don't have to tell me that.

JEREMY FORQUER: The Smell of Lilacs

I took the shortcut across the park.
The dew soaked my new suede shoes.
Through the green dusk I saw your yard light.
I could smell lilacs everywhere.
Someone was playing a piano.
That's my Stephanie Jane, I thought.
I knocked on the kitchen door.
The house was full of strangers.
They all said they didn't know you.
I walked back to the hotel.
A low branch scraped my forehead.
Sudden tears welled up in my eyes.
I should have written, should have phoned.
Three years of my life withered on the grass.
A crippled dog nipped at my heels.
I hate the smell of lilacs.

KERMIT OLMSTED: Roots

"We're staying right here the rest of our lives," I said.
"In Illinois?" she said.
"That's where we are, isn't it?" I said.

About the Author:

DAVE ETTER was born in California in 1928 and is a graduate of the University of Iowa, with a B.A. in history. Since 1959 he has been employed by a number of book publishers, including Indiana University Press, Rand McNally, and Northern Illinois University Press, where he is manuscript editor. Mr. Etter has published his poems in more than one hundred periodicals and in over forty anthologies, among them the much-acclaimed *Heartland: Poets of the Midwest.* Besides the collaborative *Voyages to the Inland Sea* (1971), Etter has published six poetry collections: *Go Read the River* (1966), *The Last Train to Prophetstown* (1968), *Strawberries* (1970), *Crabtree's Woman* (1972), *Well You Needn't* (1975), and *Bright Mississippi* (1975). He was a 1967 Bread Loaf Writers' Conference Fellow and holds several awards, including the Theodore Roethke Prize from *Poetry Northwest.* He lives in Elburn, Illinois (pop. 1100) with his wife and two children.